STUDY GUIDE

Choosing My Religion

R.C. Sproul

LIGONIER MINISTRIES
Renew your Mind.
LIGONIER.ORG | 800-435-4343

421 Ligonier Court, Sanford, FL 32771
E-mail: info@ligonier.org

Printed in the United States of America.

1

It's All Relative

INTRODUCTION

How often have you heard someone say, "That may be true for you, but it's not true for me"? This is a telltale sign of a relativist. When it comes to issues of life, ethics, religion, and God, truth for the relativist becomes a matter of expedience, preference, and whim. In this lesson, Dr. Sproul considers the impossibility of living consistently with such a worldview.

LESSON OBJECTIVES

1. To consider how relativism disregards absolute truth
2. To recognize that it is impossible for all religions to be equally true
3. To show that truth matters and ultimate truth matters ultimately

SCRIPTURE READING

Jesus answered, "My kingdom is not of this world. If my kingdom were of this world, my servants would have been fighting, that I might not be delivered over to the Jews. But my kingdom is not from the world." Then Pilate said to him, "So you are a king?" Jesus answered, "You say that I am a king. For this purpose I was born and for this purpose I have come into the world—to bear witness to the truth. Everyone who is of the truth listens to my voice." Pilate said to him, "What is truth?"

—John 18:36–38

LECTURE OUTLINE

A. The issue is truly a question of ultimate reality.

   1. We want to know what is real and true.
   2. When it comes to reality and what is true, personal feelings are not relevant.
   3. Justice and trials deal with evidence in order to determine truth.

4. That which is not real is not true.
5. Opposite ideas that are completely contradictory cannot simultaneously be true.

B. Truth or reality cannot be wrong for you and right for me.
   1. Mathematics is not relative, and neither are theology, morality, or ethics.
   2. Relativism makes truth a personal preference by espousing the idea that things that are wrong for some people might be right for others.
   3. The only absolute for relativists is that there are no absolutes.

C. Whether religion is meaningful to some and irrelevant to others does not determine the existence of God.
   1. Religious activities do not have the power to create God.
   2. Unbelief and disinterest do not have the power to kill God.

D. Several notions are commonly held in the culture today, especially by young people.
   1. God is whatever you want Him to be.
   2. All religions are equally valid and true.
   3. All religions believe in the same God.

E. It is impossible for all religions to be equally true.
   1. All religions do not believe the same things.
   2. In some cases, religions believe contradictory things.
   3. Beliefs about the personal and divine attributes of Jesus vary greatly among religions.

F. These matters arise during arguments about religion.
   1. People who do not argue about religion simply do not care.
   2. People who argue about religion care about ultimate truth.
   3. Truth matters, and ultimate truth matters ultimately.
   4. Ideas can change lives.

G. Encountering a powerful, important, catalytic reality causes people never to be the same afterward.
   1. Realizing that Jesus is real changes the whole course of one's life.
   2. Either Jesus is real or He is not real; it cannot be both.

H. The philosophy of relativism holds that all religions—or no religion at all—are equally true.
   1. Though we must reject the idea that all religions are equally true, we are called to love people regardless of their religious beliefs.
   2. It is virtuous and tolerant to think that everyone has an equal and legal right to express freely whatever religion they believe.

3. The law of this land gives us the legal right to be theologically wrong, but God never gives us the right to be wrong about Him.
4. The issue is not whether a supreme being exists but instead about who God is and what He is like.

STUDY QUESTIONS

1. Opposite ideas that are completely contradictory can simultaneously be true.
   a. True
   b. False

2. Relativism makes truth a personal preference by espousing which of the following?
   a. Only one religion is true and all the rest are false.
   b. There are absolute truths that apply to everyone.
   c. Things that are wrong for some people might be right for others.
   d. Truth always trumps personal experience.

3. Why is it impossible for all world religions to be equally true?
   a. All religions do not believe the same things.
   b. Love is not the central teaching in all religions.
   c. Racial and cultural values vary greatly.
   d. The Bible speaks of truth in all religions.

4. Coming to the conclusion that Jesus is real leads to which of the following?
   a. A change to the whole course of life
   b. A relativistic truth
   c. A religious experience that proves the reality of God
   d. Arguments about religion

5. Regardless of the various religious beliefs they encounter, what are Christians are called to do?
   a. Convert others
   b. Debate others
   c. Love others
   d. Support others

6. Which of the following rights does not God not give us?
   a. To argue about cherished beliefs
   b. To be wrong about Him
   c. To claim to possess ultimate truth
   d. To tell others that they are wrong

DISCUSSION QUESTIONS

1. How does Dr. Sproul define truth? How would you respond to someone who says that truth does not exist or that truth is relative?

2. Why do people argue about religion? Describe a time when you participated in a religious argument. Would you do anything differently?

3. How does the Constitution give us the legal right to be theologically wrong? Does God offer the same right?

4. Do people truly believe there are no absolutes? How do Christian truth, love, kindness, and patience factor into dealing with those who live in a manner that disregards absolutes?

2

The Ultimate Spring Break

INTRODUCTION

Many people believe that they owe it to themselves to indulge in sinful behavior as their reward for enduring life's daily grind. Countless people do this, but at what cost? In this lesson, Dr. Sproul shows us from Scripture how a young man's desires took him away from home so that he might enjoy the enticements of a "far country."

LESSON OBJECTIVES

1. To consider God's holiness and the sinfulness of sin
2. To recognize the extent, depth, origin, and grip of sin on humanity
3. To show how the cross is able to deliver us from sin's penalty and power

SCRIPTURE READING

And he said, "There was a man who had two sons. And the younger of them said to his father, 'Father, give me the share of property that is coming to me.' And he divided his property between them. Not many days later, the younger son gathered all he had and took a journey into a far country, and there he squandered his property in reckless living. And when he had spent everything, a severe famine arose in that country, and he began to be in need. So he went and hired himself out to one of the citizens of that country, who sent him into his fields to feed pigs. And he was longing to be fed with the pods that the pigs ate, and no one gave him anything."

—Luke 15:11–16

LECTURE OUTLINE

A. Jesus frequently taught using parables.

1. The word *parable* means to throw something alongside something else.

2. Parables are stories placed alongside teaching so that people can understand in concrete, graphic, and down-to-earth terms.

B. In the parable of the prodigal son, the son leaves the father's house after receiving his inheritance.

1. Only while the father provided benefits to the son did a relationship exist.
2. Adam and Eve similarly enjoyed benefits from God in the garden of Eden but did not enjoy God Himself, so they eventually left.
3. We do not really begin to love God until we love God for Himself and for who He is, not for what He can do for us.
4. Our prayers often consist of a list of requests for benefits from God, and when we receive such things, we tend to leave as the prodigal did.

C. The Prodigal Son left and went to a far country where no one knew him.

1. In this far country, the rules of his father did not constrain him.
2. We all need to examine what our ethics look like when we are alone and in secret.

D. Even the prodigal pagan had a conscience.

1. Even pagans know the difference between right and wrong.
2. *Prodigal* means "wasteful," and the son wasted his inheritance and wasted his life in riotous living.
3. The son squandered it all and ended up living and eating among the pigs he was tending.
4. Jesus is describing fallen man as those who leave their father and waste their lives living in a pigsty.

E. Isaiah experiences the holiness of God in his vision recorded in chapter 6.

1. The most poignant and vivid narrative of the discovery of the holiness of God is provided in Isaiah 6 as the prophet sees God high and lifted up.
2. This vision was a brilliant and blinding display of the pure holiness of God, and it caused Isaiah to fall on his face in recognition of his own sinfulness.
3. Being awakened to the character of God, Isaiah saw the vivid contrast between God's holiness and his own impurity.
4. Similarly, the Prodigal Son did not know he was in the filth of a pigsty until he remembered the riches and comfort of the father's mansion.

F. Prodigals enjoy fellowship among the pigs until we too come to such a realization.

1. We are all in this together as people of unclean mouths.
2. Even when we come to the realization that we are in a pigsty and that God disapproves of our behavior, we stay away in fear of the father's disapproval.
3. We are often too similar to the Prodigal Son. He preferred to waste his life rather than being confronted with the wrath of his father.

4. The prodigal knew enough about his father to know that in some way and to some degree the father was holy and wrathful against evil, so he stayed away.

G. This is a microcosm of the story of mankind.
   1. We are a people who cannot wait to get away from the Father's house and put distance between ourselves and the Father in order to enjoy life our way.
   2. We enjoy the benefits of the family treasure but end up preferring a pigsty to the wrath of God.
   3. Jesus understands our condition and seeks to save the lost.
   4. There is nothing we can ever keep secret from Him and no country distant enough that He cannot find us and change us.

STUDY QUESTIONS

1. The word *parable* means to throw something alongside something else.
   a. True
   b. False

2. We do not begin to love God until we love Him for which of the following?
   a. For giving us the Bible
   b. For Himself and for who He is
   c. For what He can do for us
   d. For what He can do to us

3. Where did the Prodigal Son go after leaving his father's house?
   a. The parable does not tell us
   b. To a far country
   c. To a neighboring town
   d. To live with his brother

4. What does the word *prodigal* mean?
   a. Rebellious
   b. Sinful
   c. Wandering
   d. Wasteful

5. Being awakened to the character of God, Isaiah saw the vivid contrast between which of the following?
   a. God as Creator and himself as a creature
   b. God's eternality and his own temporal nature
   c. God's holiness and his own impurity
   d. God's omniscience and his own ignorance

6. What do we typically do once we come to the realization that we are in a pigsty and that God disapproves of our behavior?
   a. Grieve
   b. Pray
   c. Repent
   d. Stay away

DISCUSSION QUESTIONS

1. What do people want from God? What do people not want from God?

2. Define *character*. When does your real character show itself?

3. Who is Jesus talking about in the parable of the prodigal son? Does being a prodigal apply more to some people than others?

4. Why did the prodigal prefer to stay in the pigsty? Describe a time when you ran off to a "far country" preferring pigsty living. How did God rescue you?

3

Whistling in the Dark

INTRODUCTION

Our lives are much like an action-drama television series—each day representing another episode that is to be continued. Too often, we act as if our last episode will not be shown. But it will, and when the show is over we must give an account to God for how we acted. Are we banking on His love and goodness to overlook our sin? Was God's wrath simply written out of the script? In this lesson, Dr. Sproul shows us how we've misunderstood God's character, and until we understand it, we are simply "whistling in the dark."

LESSON OBJECTIVES

1. To consider how wrath is consistent with a holy God
2. To recognize that God saves us from Himself and His wrath that is to come
3. To show that God's justice can only be satisfied by Christ

SCRIPTURE READING

Therefore you have no excuse, O man, every one of you who judges. For in passing judgment on another you condemn yourself, because you, the judge, practice the very same things. We know that the judgment of God rightly falls on those who practice such things. Do you suppose, O man—you who judge those who practice such things and yet do them yourself—that you will escape the judgment of God? Or do you presume on the riches of his kindness and forbearance and patience, not knowing that God's kindness is meant to lead you to repentance? But because of your hard and impenitent heart you are storing up wrath for yourself on the day of wrath when God's righteous judgment will be revealed.

—Romans 2:1–5

LECTURE OUTLINE

A. The Bible speaks of salvation at times in terms of *rescue*.

1. The Bible speaks of salvation in many different ways.
2. Israel celebrated salvation that had nothing to do with their souls going to heaven or being reconciled with God, but rather with rescue from military defeat.
3. Jesus often told sick people that their faith saved them. This may have referred to their being saved from the judgment of God or to their being saved from their disease.
4. When the Bible speaks about salvation in the highest sense, it simply means rescue from any danger or calamity.

B. There is a worse form of calamity and wrath that requires rescue.

1. When the Bible talks about salvation, it talks about rescue from the worst of all possible calamities.
2. God the Father instigates, plans, and initiates salvation by saving us from Himself and from the wrath that is to come.
3. God promises wrath by announcing an appointed day in which He is going to judge the whole world.
4. There is no concept in theology more repugnant to modern America than the idea of divine wrath.

C. The wrath of God is good.

1. We have forgotten what it means to be good because if God is really good, He has no option but wrath.
2. A just and holy judge who winks at evil, never manifests displeasure at evil, and refuses to punish evil is not a good judge.
3. Wrath is totally consistent with a holy God.
4. It should come as no surprise for us to be under God's wrath when we have repeatedly, continuously, and callously disobeyed Him, who is absolutely perfect, righteous, and holy.

D. God's holiness is part and parcel with His wrath.

1. God does not grade on a curve, and His mercy is not infinite.
2. If God is holy, wrath is the necessary consequence.
3. For the time being, God is patient, kind, and merciful as He waits for us to come to Him in repentance.
4. There is a saturation point where wrath is built up and a person is finished and without hope as God abandons those who will spend eternity in hell.

E. Mankind has yet to master handling the subjective feeling of guilt.

1. We do everything in our power to deny or minimize our guilt.

2. When denying our guilt does not work, we attempt to deny the wrath and justice of God.
3. There is only one way for the unjust and unholy to escape the wrath of God, and that is by God's satisfying His own wrath and the demands of His justice.
4. God never negotiates His character or relinquishes His holiness in order to save people. He will not abandon His righteousness to pluck prodigals out of the pigsty.

F. Our being rescued and forgiven does not mean that God has waived the requirements of holiness.
   1. Redemption after the fall makes the cross not an option but a moral necessity.
   2. God's demonstration of mercy does not involve His eliminating justice but instead involves His holy mercy in satisfying His own justice.
   3. The cross represents the satisfaction of the righteousness of God.

G. God's wrath will be satisfied one way or another.
   1. If there is no God, we do not need Jesus. If there is a holy God and we are holy ourselves, we still do not need Jesus.
   2. But if God is and God is holy, and we are not holy, then there is nothing in this universe we need more desperately than Jesus.
   3. There are only two ways that God's justice can be satisfied with respect to our sins: either we satisfy it or Christ satisfies it.
   4. Either we embrace the satisfaction of the wrath of God that Christ has made on our behalf on the cross or we will surely face His wrath ourselves.

STUDY QUESTIONS

1. In the Bible, salvation means rescue from any danger or calamity.
   a. True
   b. False

2. When it comes to salvation, God the Father instigates, plans, and does which of the following?
   a. Hopes
   b. Initiates
   c. Responds
   d. Waits

3. A judge who winks at evil, never manifests displeasure at evil, and refuses to punish evil is not a good judge.
   a. True
   b. False

4. If God is holy, which of the following is true?
   a. Wrath is based upon our works.
   b. Wrath is to be expected.
   c. Wrath is unjust.
   d. Wrath is unnecessary.

5. When denying our guilt does not work, we attempt to do which of the following?
   a. Deny that God exists
   b. Deny wrath and minimize the justice of God
   c. Maximize the wrath and minimize the justice of God
   d. Maximize the wrath and the justice of God

6. If God is and God is holy, and we are not holy, then which of the following is true?
   a. God will forgive us as long as we are sincere.
   b. Mercy will be infinite and justice will be eliminated.
   c. There is nothing we need more desperately than Jesus.
   d. We must work to be holy enough to be accepted.

DISCUSSION QUESTIONS

1. What is the greatest calamity from which any person can be rescued? Describe some ways that people "whistle in the dark" believing they have no need of Jesus?

2. What does God save us from? How would you explain this to someone who seeks to be saved solely to escape earthly pain and suffering or to be with their deceased loved ones?

3. What attribute of God makes His wrath necessary? If God is truly loving, why can He not lower His standard of perfection?

4. What are two ways God's justice can be satisfied? Describe how someone might minimize God's justice and their own guilt.

4

Rude Awakening

INTRODUCTION

The Bible says that all have sinned, and all who have sinned are spiritually dead. How can we be awakened from this death? Sin has left us in a state of utter helplessness as our sin has driven us far from God, and our misery keeps us away leading us to yet more sin. How can this pattern be broken? In this lesson, Dr. Sproul answers that question in this message entitled "Rude Awakening."

LESSON OBJECTIVES

1. To consider how sin makes us spiritually dead
2. To recognize that only the power of God through His Word and Spirit can awaken us from spiritual death
3. To show that we cannot stay in a state of ongoing sin and still be considered a Christian

SCRIPTURE READING

But when he came to himself, he said, 'How many of my father's hired servants have more than enough bread, but I perish here with hunger! I will arise and go to my father, and I will say to him, "Father, I have sinned against heaven and before you. I am no longer worthy to be called your son. Treat me as one of your hired servants."' And he arose and came to his father. But while he was still a long way off, his father saw him and felt compassion, and ran and embraced him and kissed him. And the son said to him, 'Father, I have sinned against heaven and before you. I am no longer worthy to be called your son. But the father said to his servants, 'Bring quickly the best robe, and put it on him, and put a ring on his hand, and shoes on his feet. And bring the fattened calf and kill it, and let us eat and celebrate. For this my son was dead, and is alive again; he was lost, and is found.' And they began to celebrate.

—Luke 15:17–24

LECTURE OUTLINE

A. The prodigal in the pigpen

1. While the prodigal son is in a far country, morally and spiritually dead in the pigpen, God sends His Son to satisfy God's own wrath.
2. God makes the provision to restore this runaway son to his father's house.
3. Then the young man does not want to go home.

B. The prodigal's condition

1. The bible describes this condition as spiritual death and bondage to sin where there is no life or desire to go back to the father's house.
2. Because of sin, this world is full of disappointment, pain, violence, death, disease and trouble and everybody wants to be saved from all this misery.
3. The problem is that we want to be delivered or saved from our misery, but not from our sin.

C. The prodigal comes to himself

1. Dead in sin, the prodigal much like dead Lazarus did not waken himself, because the only way to be brought to life is by the power of God Himself.
2. We have as much power to awaken ourselves from spiritual death as a corpse has the power to waken himself from physical death.
3. The hearing of His word is what the Spirit uses to waken and quicken people giving them new life.

D. Real faith

1. We do not receive the benefits of Christ or the inheritance of the Father by a claim to faith or by a decision for faith, but by the possession of faith.
2. Do not believe that a you can become a Christian and never have to change because you cannot stay in the pigsty if you are a true Christian.
3. If you truly embrace the holiness of God and rejoice in the satisfaction of what Christ did for you on the cross, He will not leave you in the pigpen.

E. The carnal Christian

1. The prodigal lived with pigs therefore smelled like a pig and was not able to rid himself of the smell right away.
2. When a person becomes a Christian and goes to the father it is not the end of sin altogether but a constant struggle to break free from the pigsty.
3. We cannot stay in sin and call ourselves a Christian.

F. Going back to the father

1. The prodigal is going to confess that he has sinned against the father and against heaven and is therefore not worthy to be called a son.
2. Every time we sin against a fellow person on a horizontal level, we also commit sin on a vertical level.

3. When we violate, lie to, steal from, or injure someone unjustly, we are not only sinning against them but also sinning against God.

G. Repentance
1. The prodigal son had a prepared speech ready for his father upon returning home to display his heartfelt sorrow and humble repentance.
2. David's repentance in Psalm 51 asked God to treat him not according to His justice but rather according to His mercy.
3. We need to be awakened to the holiness of God so that instead of running and hiding from Him, we will wake up and come home to our Father.

STUDY QUESTIONS

1. We have the power to awaken ourselves from spiritual death.
    a. True
    b. False

2. People want to be rescued from their misery without which of the following?
    a. Admitting any wrongdoing
    b. Asking for forgiveness
    c. Having to give up their sin
    d. Making amends with others

3. Every time we sin against a fellow person on a horizontal level, we also do which of the following?
    a. Commit sin against God on a vertical level
    b. Commit sin against our parents on a horizontal level
    c. Commit sin against the church on a horizontal level
    d. Commit sin against society on a vertical level

4. We are not redeemed by a profession of faith but by which of the following?
    a. A decision of faith
    b. A possession of faith
    c. A prayer of faith
    d. A promise of faith

5. We cannot call ourselves Christians if we are characterized by which of the following?
    a. Generous tithing
    b. Living a righteous and moral life
    c. Regular church attendance
    d. Remaining in a carnal lifestyle of sin

6. David's repentance in Psalm 51 asked God to treat him in which of the following way?
   a. According to His justice and according to His mercy
   b. According to His justice but not according to His mercy
   c. Not according to His justice but rather according to His mercy
   d. Not according to His justice and not according to His mercy

DISCUSSION QUESTIONS

1. Why did the prodigal stay in the pigpen? Describe a time when you delayed in turning to the Father and the eventual results.

2. How can someone know if they have a true possession of faith?

3. What does it take for us to be awakened by God? How would you respond to someone who says their awakening was a result of their prayer or decision?

4. What did the prodigal do that showed true repentance? What are other possible signs of sincere repentance?

5

Asleep in the Light

INTRODUCTION

The world is not merely indifferent toward God; the world hates God. His holiness is repugnant to those who are not holy. We love sin, and the greatest enemy of sin is holiness. Therefore, when the unregenerate person hears that God is holy, it doesn't ignite a sense of awe and delight within him but a sense of hate and hostility. Even professing Christians can succumb to the tendency to re-create the character of God in our minds and worship a god who is altogether different from the God revealed in Scripture. But God is not ashamed of His character. In fact, He calls us to imitate Him in His holiness. In this lesson, Dr. Sproul considers God's holiness as the foundation of His praiseworthiness, explaining that if God's holiness doesn't awaken a sense of awe within us, then we remain spiritual corpses.

LESSON OBJECTIVES

1. To consider how human nature at its root is hostile and hateful toward God
2. To recognize that the greatest enemy of sin is holiness
3. To show that holiness is the most fundamental attribute defining God

SCRIPTURE READING

Therefore, preparing your minds for action, and being sober-minded, set your hope fully on the grace that will be brought to you at the revelation of Jesus Christ. As obedient children, do not be conformed to the passions of your former ignorance, but as he who called you is holy, you also be holy in all your conduct, since it is written, "You shall be holy, for I am holy."

—1 Peter 1:13–16

LECTURE OUTLINE

A. God is both great and good,

1. One word that the Bible uses to point to God's greatness and goodness is the word *holy*.
2. Holiness is the most basic and fundamental attribute of God.
3. The angels sing in His presence every day the words "Holy, holy, holy."

B. God's name is to be hallowed.

1. When Jesus taught His disciples to pray, He began by regarding the Father's name as holy and hallowed.
2. Jesus wants us to wake up to who the Father is by understanding that He is holy and He will never negotiate or relinquish His holiness.
3. But we are often sound asleep and have no regard, reverence, worship, adoration, or praise for His holiness.

C. The idea of God's holiness is repugnant to those who are not holy.

1. Some people cannot stand the idea that God is holy.
2. Focusing on the holiness of God will divide people because no one is neutral about God's holiness; one will either love God's claim to holiness or hate it.
3. If there is no delight in our souls for the holiness of God, then we are spiritually dead and do not know or love God.

D. The God of holiness is worthy of our praise.

1. In our sin, we do not and cannot delight in God because He is holy and we are not.
2. Our only hope is that this universe is governed by an all-powerful, all-holy God who will never use His power in a way that is inconsistent with His character.
3. God's holiness is the foundation for God's praiseworthiness. A God who is not holy is not worthy of praise.

E. Human nature at its root is hostile and hateful toward God.

1. We are sworn enemies of the Almighty because our fall is so great and our corruption so profound that we will not have God in our reprobate minds.
2. Indifference toward God is contempt for His very being.

F. The human heart is an idol factory.

1. We often strip God of His holiness, take away His justice, remove His wrath, and conjure up a god who is only love, kindness, mercy, and grace.
2. Substituting such an idol for the real God reveals the depth of our hostility to the God who is.
3. Even Christians run from the holiness and sovereignty of God, because they do not want a God who is sovereign except when they need something.

G. The greatest enemy of sin is holiness.
   1. If God is holy, then humanity is in trouble.
   2. We are not holy and we know it; therefore, we want to push God out of our minds.
   3. We do not like to think about our sin and His holiness, but if we want life, we must come to grips with both concepts.

H. What should we do with our guilt?
   1. When we sin, there is a real sense in which we are left naked and in need of the covering that God has prepared for His people at the cross.
   2. We must put our trust in Christ alone to cover us, because it is Christ alone who can bring us back into fellowship with a holy God.
   3. Christ lived a life of perfect righteousness and He has given that righteousness to all who will embrace Him in faith.

STUDY QUESTIONS

1. When we have been awakened to a sense of the majesty of God, we will never go back to sleep.
   a. True
   b. False

2. Which word does the Bible use to point to God's greatness and to His goodness?
   a. Holy
   b. Omnipotent
   c. Sovereign
   d. Transcendent

3. Which of the following is true of God?
   a. He will increase in His holiness.
   b. He will never negotiate His holiness.
   c. His holiness outweighs His omniscience.
   d. His grace outweighs His holiness.

4. Human nature at its root is which of the following?
   a. Fearful of God
   b. Hateful toward God
   c. Loving toward God
   d. Loving toward others

5. We tend to push God out of our minds because we have trouble facing which two things?
   a. Death and hell
   b. God's wrath and judgment
   c. Our finiteness and God's infiniteness
   d. Our sin and God's holiness

6. Because God is holy, we can do which of the following?
   a. Be moral
   b. Commune with Him
   c. Delight in Him
   d. Pray to Him

DISCUSSION QUESTIONS

1. Describe a time when you had a vivid sense of the presence of God. What was your initial response?

2. Why is the subject of God's holiness so divisive and controversial? Why do people often reject the holiness and sovereignty of God?

3. What is the most basic attribute of God? How does this attribute affect all of the other attributes of God?

4. How does God's holiness relate to our sin and guilt? What is it about God's holiness that makes Him worthy of praise?

STUDY QUESTIONS ANSWER KEY

Lesson 1

1. b
2. c
3. a
4. a
5. c
6. b

Lesson 2

1. a
2. b
3. b
4. d
5. c
6. d

Lesson 3

1. a
2. b
3. a
4. b
5. b
6. c

Lesson 4

1. b
2. c
3. a
4. b
5. d
6. c

Lesson 5

1. b
2. a
3. b
4. b
5. d
6. c

STUDY QUESTION EXPLANATIONS

LESSON 1:

1. The law of noncontradiction states that opposite ideas that are completely contradictory cannot simultaneously be true. While relativists say they accept contradictory truth claims, basic logic and reality point out the problems of accepting such claims.

2. Relativism makes truth a personal preference by stating that things that are wrong for some people might be right for others. The only absolute for relativists is that there are no absolutes. "Nothing is true for everyone" is the foundation of relativism.

3. It is impossible for all religions to be equally true because all religions do not believe the same things. In some cases, religions believe in contradictory things. For example, beliefs about the personal and divine attributes of Jesus greatly vary among world religions.

4. Whether religion is meaningful to some and irrelevant to others does not determine the existence of God. Encountering a powerful, important, catalytic reality causes people never to be the same afterward. And realizing that Jesus is real changes the whole course of one's life for now and for eternity.

5. It is virtuous and tolerant to think that everyone has an equal and legal right to express freely whatever religion they believe. Christians are called to love people regardless of their religious beliefs. We can vigorously debate and defend Christianity with people and try to convince them of biblical realities, but love, patience, and kindness need to be evident in conveying truth.

6. Every religion is not equally true or equally valid. While the law of our land gives us the legal right to be theologically wrong, God never gives us the right to be wrong about Him. The issue is not about whether a supreme being exists but instead about who God is and what He is like.

LESSON 2:

1. Jesus frequently taught using parables. The word *parable* means to throw something alongside something else. Parables are stories places alongside teaching so that people can understand in concrete, graphic, and down-to-earth terms.

2. Like the Prodigal Son, Adam and Eve enjoyed benefits from God in the garden of Eden but did not enjoy God Himself, so they eventually left. We do not

really begin to love God until we love Him for Himself and for who He is, not for what He can do for us.

3. The Prodigal Son left and went to a far country where no one knew him and the rules of his father did not constrain him. The real question that we all need to face is what our ethics are like when we are alone and in secret. The son did not want to be watched or accountable.

4. *Prodigal* means "wasteful," and the son wasted his inheritance and wasted his life in riotous living. He squandered it all and ended up living and eating among pigs. Jesus is describing fallen man as those who leave their father and waste their lives living in a pigsty.

5. Isaiah's vision was a brilliant and blinding display of the pure holiness of God, which caused Isaiah to fall on his face in recognition of his own sinfulness. Being awakened to the character of God, Isaiah saw the vivid contrast between God's holiness and his own impurity.

6. When we realize that we are in a pigsty and that God disapproves of our behavior, we stay away in fear of the father's disapproval. Like the Prodigal Son, we would rather waste our lives than be confronted with the wrath of the Father, who is holy and wrathful against evil.

LESSON 3:

1. While the Bible speaks of salvation in many different ways, its most rudimentary meaning refers to being rescued from any danger or calamity. For example, Israel celebrated salvation that had nothing to do with their souls' going to heaven or their being reconciled with God. It had to do with their being rescued from the calamity of military defeat.

2. God the Father instigates, plans, and initiates salvation. God is the author of salvation and commands us to be saved yet promises wrath by announcing an appointed a day in which He is going to judge the whole world.

3. A just and holy judge who winks at evil, never manifests displeasure at evil and refuses to punish evil is not a good judge. It should come as no surprise for us to be under God's wrath when we have repeatedly, continuously, and callously disobeyed Him, who is absolutely perfect, righteous, and holy.

4. If God is holy, wrath is to be expected. For the time being, God is patient, kind, and merciful as He waits for us to come to Him and repent. There is a saturation point where wrath is built up and a person is without hope as God abandons those who will spend eternity in hell.

5. We do everything in our power to deny or minimize our guilt. When that does not work, we attempt to deny the wrath and justice of God. God will never negotiate His own character or ever stop being holy just to save us because He will not abandon His own righteousness.

6. If God is and God is holy, and we are not holy, there is nothing in this universe we need more desperately than Jesus. Either we embrace the satisfaction of the wrath of God that Christ has made on our behalf on the cross or we will surely face it on our own.

LESSON 4:

1. Dead in sin, the prodigal much like Lazarus did not waken himself, because the only way to be brought to life is by the power of God Himself. We have as much power to awaken ourselves from spiritual death as a corpse has the power to awaken himself from physical death.

2. Because of sin, this world is full of disappointment, pain, violence, death, disease and trouble and everybody wants to be saved from all this misery. Like the prodigal son, the problem is that we often want to be rescued from our misery, but not necessarily from our sin.

3. Every time we sin against a fellow person on a horizontal level, we also commit sin on a vertical level. When we violate, lie to, steal from, or injure someone unjustly, we are not only sinning against them but also sinning against God.

4. To have real salvation, one must have real faith. The threat of God's judgment is real. The satisfaction of His justice by Christ is real. We do not receive the benefits of Christ or the inheritance of the Father by a claim to faith or by a decision for faith, but by the possession of faith.

5. The prodigal lived with pigs therefore smelled like a pig and was not able to rid himself of the smell right away. When becoming a Christian, it is not the end of sin altogether but a constant struggle to break free from the pigsty. We cannot stay in sin and call ourselves a Christian.

6. The prodigal exhibited repentance like David did in Psalm 51 when asking God to treat him not according to His justice but rather according to His mercy. The prodigal asked for mercy and to be a servant since he felt unworthy to be called a son.

LESSON 5:

1. Even though we have been awakened to a sense of the majesty of God, we often go back to sleep. We need to be continually awakened to the character and holiness of God. Meeting God is never boring, and if it is, we have not really met Him.

2. The word that the Bible uses to point to God's greatness and to His goodness is the word *holy*. Holiness is the most basic and fundamental characteristic or attribute defining God as illustrated by the angels' singing in His presence every day the words "Holy, holy, holy."

3. When Jesus taught His disciples to pray, He began with regarding the Father's name as holy and hallowed. Jesus wants us to wake up to who the Father is by understanding that He is holy, He will never negotiate His holiness, and He will never stop being holy.

4. Human nature at its root is hostile and hateful toward God. We are sworn enemies of the Almighty because our fall is so great and our corruption so profound that we will not have God in our reprobate minds. Any indifference toward God is contempt for His very being.

5. The greatest enemy of sin is holiness. If God is holy, then we are in trouble, because we are not holy and we know it. Therefore, we want to push God out of our minds. We do not like to think about our sin and His holiness, but if we want life, we have to face those two things.

6. The reason that we can delight in God at all is because He is holy. Our only hope is that this universe is governed by an all-powerful, all-holy God who will never use His power in an unholy way. The reason that God is praiseworthy is because He is holy.